Aquatic Invertebrate Monitoring at Wilson's Creek National Battlefield

2005-2007 Trend Report

Natural Resource Technical Report NPS/HTLN/NRTR—2010/287

David E. Bowles
National Park Service
The Heartland I&M Network and Prairie Cluster Prototype Monitoring Program
Wilson's Creek National Battlefield
6424 West Farm Road 182
Republic, Missouri 65738

February 2010

U.S. Department of the Interior
National Park Service
Natural Resource Program Center
Fort Collins, Colorado

The National Park Service, Natural Resource Program Center publishes a range of reports that address natural resource topics of interest and applicability to a broad audience in the National Park Service and others in natural resource management, including scientists, conservation and environmental constituencies, and the public.

The Natural Resource Technical Report Series is used to disseminate results of scientific studies in the physical, biological, and social sciences for both the advancement of science and the achievement of the National Park Service mission. The series provides contributors with a forum for displaying comprehensive data that are often deleted from journals because of page limitations.

All manuscripts in the series receive the appropriate level of peer review to ensure that the information is scientifically credible, technically accurate, appropriately written for the intended audience, and designed and published in a professional manner. This report received informal peer review by subject-matter experts who were not directly involved in the collection, analysis, or reporting of the data.

Views, statements, findings, conclusions, recommendations, and data in this report are those of the author(s) and do not necessarily reflect views and policies of the National Park Service, U.S. Department of the Interior. Mention of trade names or commercial products does not constitute endorsement or recommendation for use by the National Park Service.

This report is available from http://science.nature.nps.gov/im/units/htln/ and the Natural Resource Publications Management website (http://www.nature.nps.gov/publications/NRPM/).

Please cite this publication as:

NPS 410/101120, February 2010

Contents

List of Figures

List of Tables

Executive Summary

In the late 1980's, the National Park Service (NPS) began an intensive program to monitor water quality and invertebrate community structure in prairie streams at several midwestern parks. Included in this baseline study was Wilson's Creek National Battlefield (WICR). Preliminary monitoring was conducted at WICR from 1988 to 1989 at Wilson's Creek and a tributary, Skegg's Branch. Following this baseline year, monitoring was not conducted again until 1996, but it has since been conducted annually. An additional tributary, Terrell Creek, was included for monitoring beginning in 2006. Since 2006, monitoring at WICR has been based on a monitoring protocol developed by the Heartland Network using revised methodology from previous protocols. The objectives of current monitoring are to: 1) determine the status and trends of invertebrate species diversity, abundance, and community metrics, and 2) relate the invertebrate community to overall water quality through quantification of metrics related to species richness, abundance, diversity, and region-specific multi-metric indices as indicators of water quality and habitat condition.

Water quality, habitat, and invertebrate community metrics varied considerably among sampling years and streams sampled. However, it is not clear whether or not the observed variation is biologically important. Based on the invertebrate community metrics reported here, the water quality of Wilson's Creek within WICR is judged as impaired, while water quality of Skegg's Branch and Terrell Creek is judged to be generally good. Wilson's Creek is impacted from a combination of urbanization and treated effluent from a wastewater treatment plant. It is listed as a 303d stream by the Missouri Department of Natural Resources due to an unspecified contaminant. Skegg's Branch although historically having high water quality, may be starting to experience the effects of urbanization associated with the growth of Republic, Missouri where this stream originates. Because observed impairment is attributed to activities in the watersheds outside the park boundaries, there are few available options to park management for mitigating this situation. The long history and continuing efforts of aquatic invertebrate monitoring at Wilson's Creek National Battlefield provides a sound tool to recognize both deterioration and chronic decline of water quality.

Acknowledgements

I thank David Peitz, Tyler Cribbs, Gary Sullivan, Carla Stark, Hope Dodd, Jake Waters, Angela Bandy, Jan Hinsey, Mike DeBacker, Greg Wallace, Jessica Luraas, and Lloyd Morrison for assisting with this project.

Introduction

In the late 1980's, the National Park Service (NPS) began an intensive program to monitor water quality and invertebrate community structure in prairie streams at several Midwestern parks (Harris *et al.* 1991). Included in this baseline study was Wilson's Creek National Battlefield (WICR). Based on the study of Harris *et al.* (1991), a preliminary protocol was suggested by Peterson (1996), in which data dating back to 1988 and collected under the guidance described in Boyle *et al.* (1990) were analyzed. The streams monitored in this initial effort and since are Wilson's Creek and Skegg's Branch. An official invertebrate biomonitoring protocol, drawing heavily on Peterson's (1996) results, was published in 1999 (Peterson *et al.*, 1999). A revised monitoring protocol (Bowles *et al.* 2008) included invertebrate monitoring at WICR using revised methodology from Peterson *et al.* (1999). The revised protocol includes monitoring sites on Wilson's Creek and Skegg's Branch in addition to Terrell Creek, which was added as a monitoring site in 2006 after it became part of WICR in 2005.

Wilson's Creek is one of the largest tributary streams in the James River basin, draining most of the city of Springfield, Missouri. Due largely to this urban drainage, Wilson's Creek has experienced serious water quality degradation over the past few decades (Black 1997, Richards and Johnson 2002). The chronic pollution of Wilson's Creek arises from point sources such as the treatment plant and non-point sources such as stormwater run-off. Due to its urban origin, Wilson's Creek is also prone to flashiness following only moderate rainfall amounts (Richards and Johnson 2002). Historically, summer storms combined with wastewater effluent resulted in severe depletion of dissolved oxygen in Wilson's Creek (Emmett et al. 1978). However, the combined and synchronous effects of these stressors on aquatic life in Wilson's Creek are presently unknown. Below Rader Spring downstream of the City of Springfield, most of the flow of Wilson's Creek is treated effluent from the Southwest Wastewater Treatment Plant (City of Springfield). Currently about 42.5 million gallons of treated sewage is released into Wilson's Creek. Although plant upgrades done in 1977 and 2001 aimed at partial removal of phosphorus from the wastewater, it continues to produce nutrient loads that flow into Wilson's Creek (Missouri Department of Natural Resources 2007). Phosporus-and nitrogen related compounds remain relatively high in Wilson's Creek (Missouri Department of Natural Resources 2007) and at sufficient levels to stimulate algal growth (Mueller and Helsel 1996). The treatment plant presently reduces average phosphorus discharge levels to 0.5 milligrams per liter (http://www.springfieldmo.gov/sanitary/phosphorus.html). The U.S. Environmental Protection Agency (Muller and Helsel 1996) recommends that total phosphorus should not exceed 0.05 mg/L in a stream at a point where it enters a lake or reservoir, and should not exceed 0.1 mg/L in streams that do not discharge directly into lakes or reservoirs. Muller and Helsel (1996) also noted that background nitrate concentrations in streams generally are less than 0.6 mg/L. However, Missouri Department of Natural Resources (2007) reported nitrate-nitrite and total nitrogen concentrations in Wilson's Creek as 1.73 mg/l and 1.93 mg/l, respectively. However, it is not entirely clear how much of this nutrient loading comes from the treatment plant in comparison to general urban run-off from the City of Springfield.

Upgrades to the wastewater treatment plant have improved the water quality in the creek in recent years, particularly dissolved oxygen concentration (Berkas 1980, 1982). Concentrations of contaminants reported by Richards and Johnson (2002) are generally well below their respective state limits for the protection of aquatic life, but fecal indicator bacteria densities occasionally exceed the state limit for whole-body-contact recreation during base-flow conditions and can be orders of magnitude greater in stormwater samples. Despite these known pollutants, there have been no serious actions to mitigate the water quality degradation produced by urban stormwater run-off into Wilson's Creek.

Skegg's Branch flows through a largely rural, undisturbed landscape and its water quality and invertebrate community have generally maintained their integrity. However, due to relatively recent expansive growth in the City of Republic, Missouri where the small stream originates, it may be prone to degradation similar to that observed for Wilson's Creek. Terrell Creek lies in a rural watershed and receives most of its flow from a spring source (Double Spring) located within the boundaries of the battlefield.

Aquatic invertebrates are an important tool for understanding and detecting changes in ecosystem integrity over time. The monitoring objectives of this study, as described by DeBacker *et al.* (2005), are: 1) determine the status and trends of invertebrate species diversity, abundance, and community metrics, and 2) relate the invertebrate community to overall water quality through quantification of metrics related to species richness, abundance, diversity, and region-specific multi-metric indices as indicators of water quality and habitat condition. Peitz and Cribbs (2005) reported on status and trends of the aquatic invertebrate community at WICR from inception of monitoring through 2004. The purpose of this report is to summarize aquatic invertebrate monitoring data collected from 2005-2007 under the framework of the revised monitoring protocol and assess that data with respect to trend since the inception of monitoring in 1989.

Methods

Methods and procedures used in this report follow Bowles *et al.* (2008), Monitoring Protocol for Aquatic Invertebrates of Small Streams in the Heartland Inventory & Monitoring Network. Samples were collected from Wilson's Creek, Skegg's Branch, and Terrell Creek (Figure 1).

For each sample, current velocity (meters/second) and depth (cm) were recorded directly in front of the sampling net frame. Qualitative habitat variables (percent embeddedness, periphyton, filamentous algae, aquatic vegetation, deposition, and organic material) were estimated within the sampling net frame as percentage categories (0, <10, 10-40, 40-75, >75). Habitat data were analyzed as midpoints of each category. Dominant substrate size from the area within the sampling net frame was visually assessed using the Wentworth scale (Wentworth 1922). Habitat variables and dominant substrate size were collected only during 2006-2007. Stream discharge was measured upstream of the sampling site after invertebrate collections were completed in 2007. Discharge was not measured in 2005, and the data presented were obtained from the US Geological Survey Water Resources database (http://waterdata.usgs.gov/nwis). Water quality data for 2005 represent static readings taken from each sampled riffle with calibrated hand-held meters. In comparison, water quality readings for 2006-2007 were recorded hourly at least 24 hours prior to sampling for each stream using calibrated data loggers or sondes. Due to equipment failure, no data for dissolved oxygen and pH were collected at some sites in 2007. The water quality data presented in this report are only intended to describe the prevailing conditions that influence the structure of invertebrate communities. These data may help explain variability between sampling periods, but they should not be used as an analytical tool in the strictest sense (Bowles *et al.* 2008). Moreover, the water quality data represent only a snap-shot of the broad temporal range of conditions, and should be cautiously interpreted. Due to the limitations of using water quality data obtained with data loggers, the invertebrate community is used here as a surrogate of the long-term water quality condition of WICR streams.

For each stream, three successive riffles were sampled with three benthic invertebrate samples collected at each riffle, resulting in nine samples per stream. A Surber stream bottom sampler (500 μm mesh, 0.093 m^2) was used to collect the samples. Samples were sorted in the laboratory following a subsampling routine described in Bowles *et al.* (2008). Taxa were identified to the lowest practical taxonomic level (usually genus) and counted. The Missouri Stream Condition Index (SCI) was calculated for each stream (Sarver et al. 2002). This multi-metric index is based on the scores of four independent metrics including taxa richness, EPT richness, Shannon Index, and the biotic index.

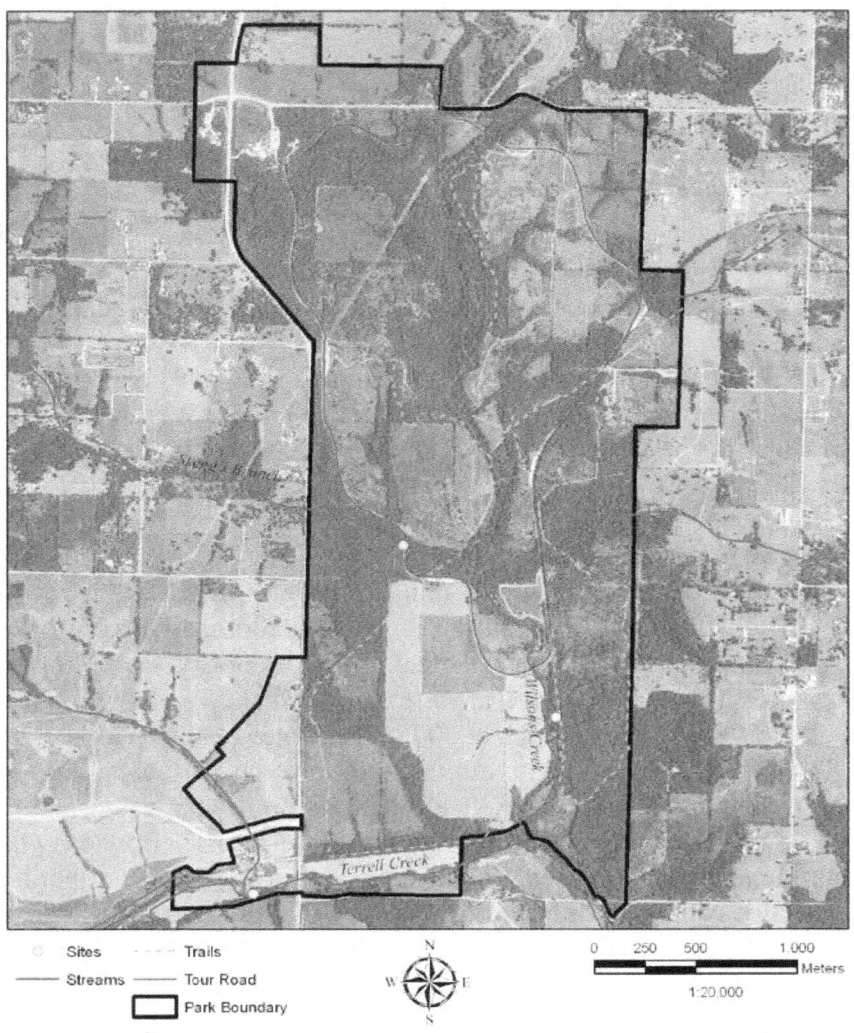

Figure 1. Aquatic invertebrate monitoring sites (yellow dots) at Wilson's Creek National Battlefield.

The primary interest in the analysis and interpretation of the data presented in this report is the magnitude of change rather than change *per se* (Bowles *et al*. 2008), and whether it represents something biologically important. Null hypothesis significance testing in the strict sense may not be the best approach given these goals (Morrison 2007). Therefore, univariate control charts were established to illustrate the general trend of invertebrate community metrics and provide a visual tool for managers to determine which variables may require more in-depth analyses or management action in the future. Control charts plot a characteristic through time with reference to its expected value. Upper or lower thresholds specify amounts of variability beyond what would normally be expected and indicate when a system is going 'out of control' (Morrison 2008). Control charts as used here contain a control limit of (mean ± 1.86 standard deviations for Wilson's Creek and mean ± 2.02 for Skegg's Branch) for those community metrics that respectively decrease or increase due to stressors. This threshold serves as an indicator to suggest biologically important change may be occurring. Setting a control chart threshold equal to 1.86 and 2.02 standard deviations, respectively, is analogous to significance tests at a critical value of 0.05 for one-tailed tests (since we are only interested in change in one direction). The student's t-distribution (df = 8 Wilson's Creek, df = 5 Skegg's Branch) was used to determine the one-tailed area because of the relatively small sample size. A critical value of 0.05 is widely accepted as the 'standard' in significance testing approaches. Control limits may need to be reset after more data are accumulated.

Data from 1996-2004 serve as a baseline for constructing thresholds based on standard deviations of the mean of these data points. This period was chosen because the methods used were most similar to those used in Peterson et al. (1999) and the current protocol. It is not completely clear if the data collected prior to 1996 followed this guidance. The data addressed in this report are only those collected during the May-June index period from the general sampling reach described in Bowles *et al.* (2008). It does not include all historical data summarized in Peitz and Cribbs (2005). A critical value of 0.05 indicates that one out of every 20 data points will exceed this limit if the population is not changing, which is the assumption. Thus, the primary purpose of sampling to date with respect to control chart construction has been to establish a baseline and evaluate natural variability. Data collected from 2005-2007 are evaluated against this baseline period.

Results

Water Quality and Habitat

Core 5 water quality measurements (Table 1) varied considerably among streams and there was modest variation among years for each stream. Observed differences among streams are likely due to their individual physical characteristics and other factors. For example, a longer deployment time of the dataloggers in 2006 resulted in Page: 7 substantially more readings compared to 2005 and 2007. The longer loggers are left out, the larger the range of variability they are likely to record. Wilson's Creek had higher water temperatures and specific conductance in comparison to Skegg's Branch and Terrell Creek. Values for specific conductance were typically well above acceptable ranges for regional streams (Table 2). Mean turbidity recorded for Wilson's Creek in 2006-2007 was also within the acceptable range for the region, but the range of data included values that were well above acceptable limits. The higher observed readings at Wilson's Creek for temperature, specific conductance, and turbidity likely are due to the effects of urbanization in this watershed, and because most of the base flow for Wilson's Creek comes from the discharge of the Southwest Wastewater Treatment Plant in Springfield. The urbanized watershed of Wilson's Creek also produces a dynamic hydrograph (i.e., flashy flows) and the creek becomes very turbid following only a light rainfall (*e.g.*, <2 cm). The water quality data for Skegg's Branch and Terrell Creek were generally typical for regional streams and do not suggest impairment based on the acceptable ranges in Table 2.

Discharge (Table 3) for the respective streams was substantially higher in 2007 compared to 2006, and 2005 for Wilson's Creek. Discharge estimates are intended to illustrate the general flow tendencies for the respective streams for a given sampling year and are not intended to be precise measurements. Wilson's and Terrell creeks were similar in depth at riffles sampled, but Skegg's Branch was considerably shallower (Figure 2). Current velocities associated with samples taken in Wilson's Creek were roughly double those recorded for the other two streams. In some cases velocities in Wilson's Creek approached 1 m/sec (Figure 3).

Although habitat parameters were generally consistent between years for a given stream, there was considerable variation observed among the streams. Embeddedness, or the degree to which fine sediments surround coarse substrates on the surface of a streambed, averaged around 25% for Wilson's Creek (Figure 4) but typically exceeded 30% for Skegg's Branch (Figure 5) and Terrell Creek (Figure 6). Filamentous algae was poorly represented in riffles of all three streams although we observed substantial algal growth in Wilson's Creek between riffles. Aquatic plants were poorly represented in Wilson's Creek (<32%) while Skegg's Branch and Terrell Creek both had much greater aquatic plant growth (45-50%, respectively). The denser vegetation in the latter two streams probably relates to their respective base flows being dominated by springs and their watersheds being largely rural in location. The dominant aquatic vegetation in Skegg's Branch was mosses, while Terrell Creek had a diverse assemblage of mosses and hydrophytes. Periphyton consistently averaged about 25% in samples for all three streams. Mean deposition was moderate at all sites and ranged from 30-48%, which is indicative of the relatively low gradient of these streams. In contrast, mean organic material composition in the sampling areas was relatively low for Wilson's and Terrell creeks (≤25%), but it was slightly higher for Skegg's Branch (20-33%). The higher organic content observed for Skegg's Branch likely reflects the denser riparian canopy and associated allochthonous inputs for this stream. Mean substrate sizes among riffles and streams were similar and the overlap of standard error bars shows that substrate sizes overlapped broadly among the three streams (Figure 7).

Invertebrate Community Metrics

Invertebrate metrics were highly variable among streams and years sampled (Tables 4-6, Figures 8-23). Particularly notable is the wide range in number of families collected among years ranging from a high of 12 to a low of 8. However, since 1999 the number of families represented in samples has remained relatively consistent. Because streams are highly variable ecosystems, observed differences in sampling metrics among years likely is not biologically significant.

Data for Skegg's Branch also was highly variable, but there was a notable decrease in family richness and EPT ratio across years indicating more tolerant Chironomidae are becoming more prevalent. These metrics suggest water quality in Skegg's Branch may have declined since data were first collected in 1988-1989. However, the variability in the data does not permit a definitive assessment of impairment. Although Shannon index scores reported here for all streams are relatively low (≤ 2.69), they are comparable with those of other regional systems (Jones *et al*. 1981, Bowles *et al*. 2008). Mean HBI scores were consistently around 5 or 6 for Wilson's Creek and Skegg's Branch, indicating that taxa represented in samples were, on average, moderately tolerant of pollution. The preliminary data for Terrell Creek are insufficient to judge condition of that resource, but the metrics in general suggest this stream has high water quality.

SCI scores calculated for Wilson's Creek ranged from 8 to 10, and has not dropped below 10 since 2001 (Table 4). SCI scores for Skegg's Branch ranged from 10 to 14, but they have not exceeded 12 since 1999, and scores for Terrell Creek for 2006-2007 were 18 and 14, respectively (Tables 5-6). SCI scores of 16-20 indicate no impairment, 10-14 indicate impaired conditions, while scores ranging from 4-8 indicate a very impaired stream condition. The highly variable SCI scores are a direct reflection of the highly variable individual metrics that comprise them.

Control charts for Wilson's Creek and Skegg's Branch showed that few of the invertebrate metrics exceeded their respective control limits. For Wilson's Creek, EPT richness was highly variable with respect to the control limit, which was exceeded on numerous occasions. In 2007, the mean value for HBI exceeded the control limit although the range of data included values that did not exceed the limit. Metric values for Skegg's Branch were variable but in general did not exceed the control limit. Two exception for Skegg's Branch were Shannon index (families) in 2005 and EPT ratio in 2007. Control charts were not prepared for Terrell Creek because monitoring has only been conducted there for two years.

Table 1. Water quality data for streams at Wilson's Creek National Battlefield, 2005-2007. Data in 2005 were collected with hand-held instruments. Data for 2006-2007 were collected continuously with calibrated data loggers. Values are mean, standard deviation, and range.

Year	Stream	N		Temperature (°C)	Specific Conductance (μm/cm)	Dissolved Oxygen (mg/liter)	pH	Turbidity (NTU)
2005	Wilson's Creek	9	Mean	19.82	774.4	9.23	7.51	n/a
			Standard Deviation	0.26	4.16	0.12	0.08	n/a
			Range	19.5-20.1	770-781	9.11-9.41	7.44-7.64	n/a
	Skegg's Branch	9	Mean	16.42	399	9.254	7.434	n/a
			Standard Deviation	0.15	1.73	0.14	0.12	n/a
			Range	16.2-16.6	396-400	9.08-9.37	7.31-7.58	n/a
2006	Wilson's Creek	139	Mean	22.49	486.48	9.16	7.77	9.57
			Standard Deviation	1.49	51.61	1.42	0.17	28.20
			Range	18.96-25.13	348-563	7.45-12.13	7.43-8.11	0-300.5
	Skegg's Branch	139	Mean	18.68	495.83	8.82	7.92	0.69
			Standard Deviation	1.77	7.39	1.20	0.06	0.55
			Range	14.38-21.67	480-505	7.1-11.55	7.82-8.07	0-3.7
	Terrell Creek	90	Mean	16.25	471.68	8.98	7.38	2.70
			Standard Deviation	0.86	2.24	1.45	0.07	2.08
			Range	15.37-18.09	467-474	7.49-11.8	7.29-7.51	0-7.1
2007	Wilson's Creek	26	Mean	18.49	642.96	n/a	n/a	4.25
			Standard Deviation	1.33	14.02	n/a	n/a	0.64
			Range	17.05-20.89	624-665	n/a	n/a	3.1-5.1
	Skegg's Branch	90	Mean	15.27	489.51	n/a	n/a	2.07
			Standard Deviation	0.86	15.34	n/a	n/a	0.64
			Range	14.36-17.26	453-511	n/a	n/a	1.1-3.7
	Terrell Creek	25	Mean	14.70	477.64	6.45	n/a	0.76
			Standard Deviation	0.32	1.82	0.58	n/a	0.19
			Range	14.28-15.28	475-481	5.79-7.47	n/a	0.5-1.3

Table 2. Acceptable ranges for water quality parameters in southwestern Missouri streams. Adapted from Brown and Czarnezki (undated).

Water Quality Parameter	Acceptable Range
Temperature	0-34 °C
Dissolved Oxygen	5-15 mg/liter
Specific Conductance	100-400 µS/cm
pH	6.5-9.0
Turbidity	Variable, but generally <10 NTU dry weather

Table 3. Discharge for streams at Wilson's Creek National Battlefield, 2005-2007. Data from 2005 are from: http://waterdata.usgs.gov/nwis/

Year	Wilson's Creek	Skegg's Branch	Terrell Creek
2005	1.16	n/a	n/a
2006	0.93	0.01	0.10
2007	4.56	0.14	0.56

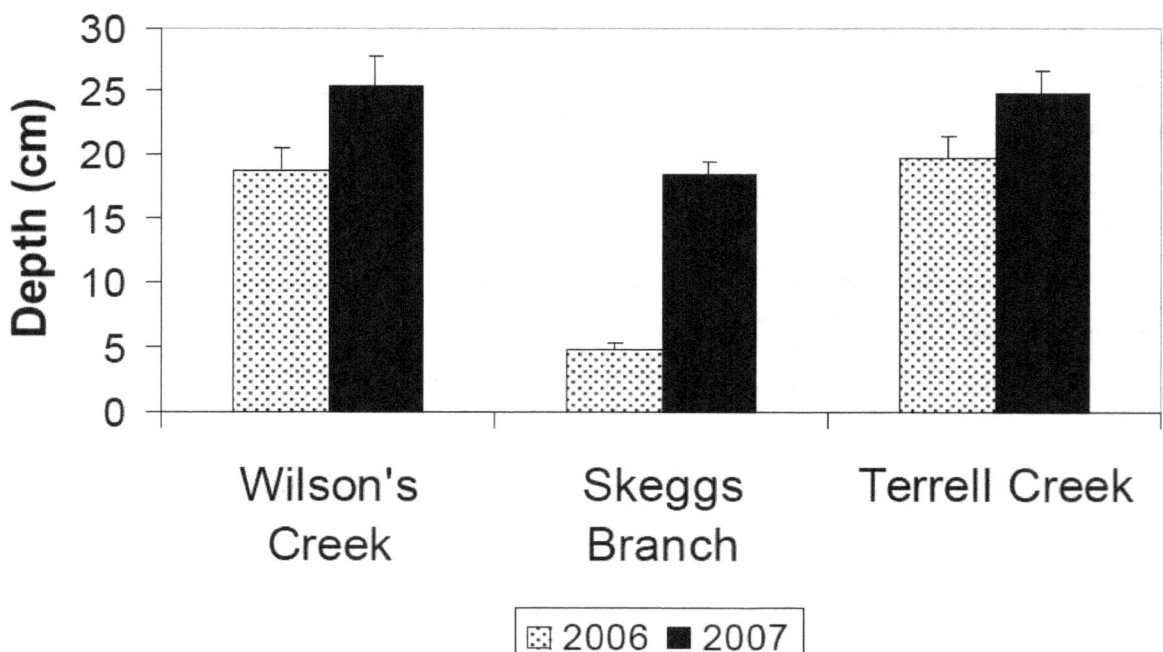

Figure 2. Mean depth (cm) and standard errors of riffles where benthic samples were collected.

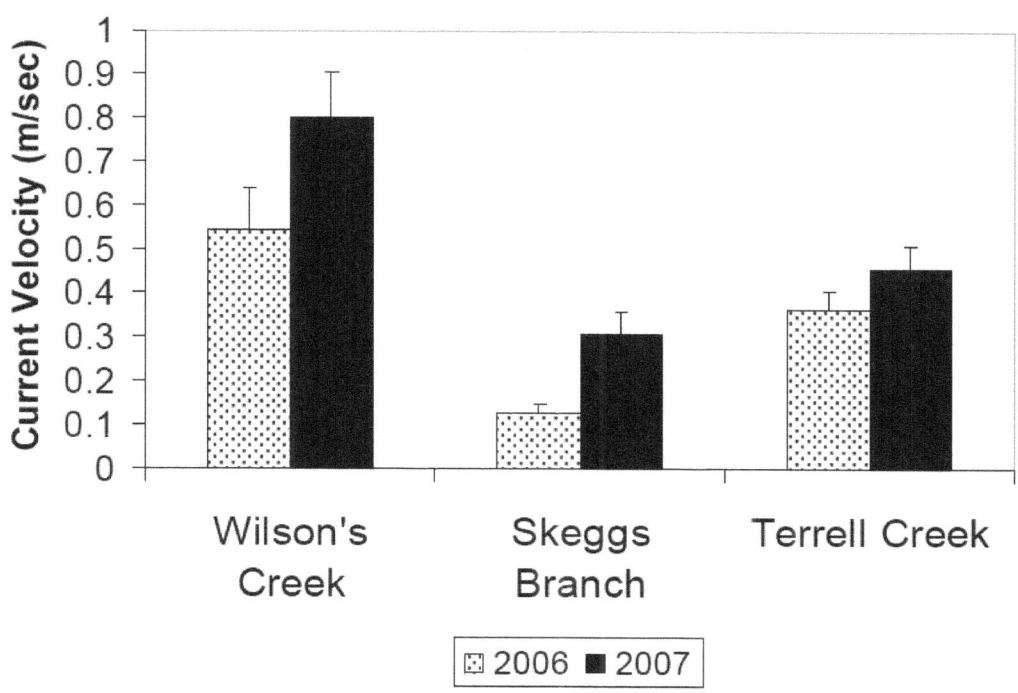

Figure 3. Mean current velocity (m/sec) and standard errors of riffles where benthic samples were collected.

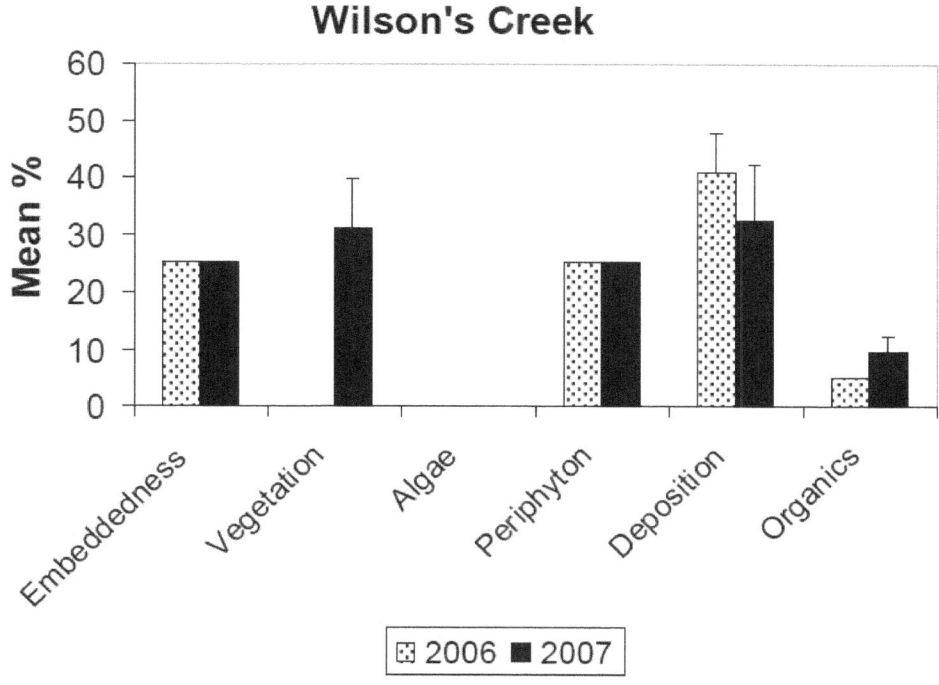

Figure 4. Mean percent and standard errors of habitat parameters associated with benthic samples in Wilson's Creek, Wilson's Creek National Battlefield, 2006-2007.

11

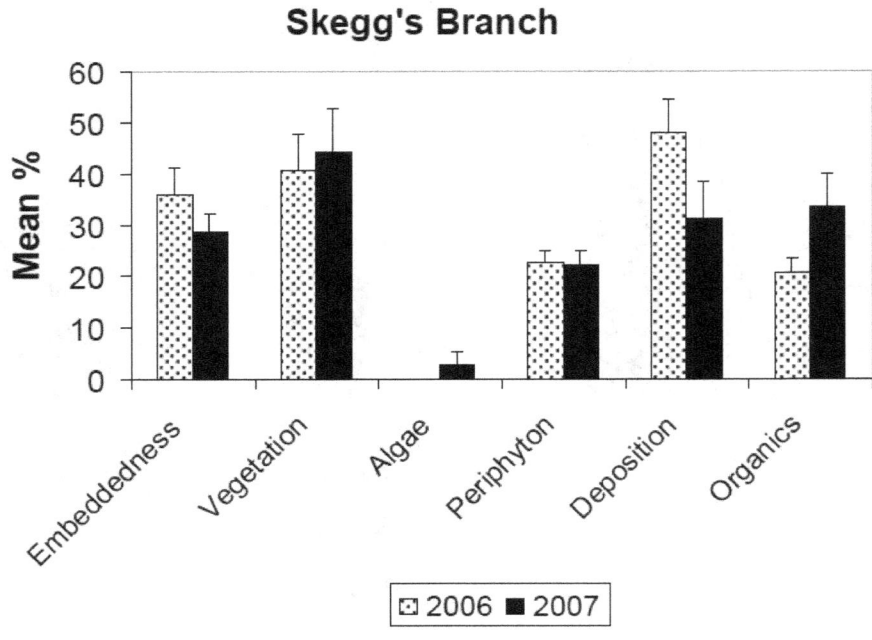

Figure 5. Mean percent and standard errors of habitat parameters associated with benthic samples in Skegg's Branch, Wilson's Creek National Battlefield, 2006-2007.

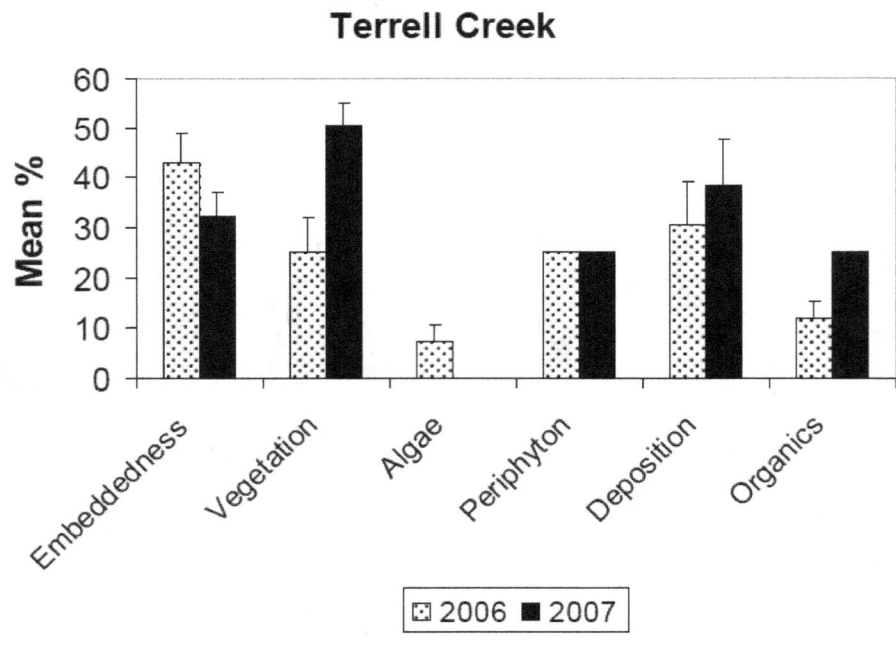

Figure 6. Mean percent and standard errors of habitat parameters associated with benthic samples in Terrell Creek, Wilson's Creek National Battlefield, 2006-2007.

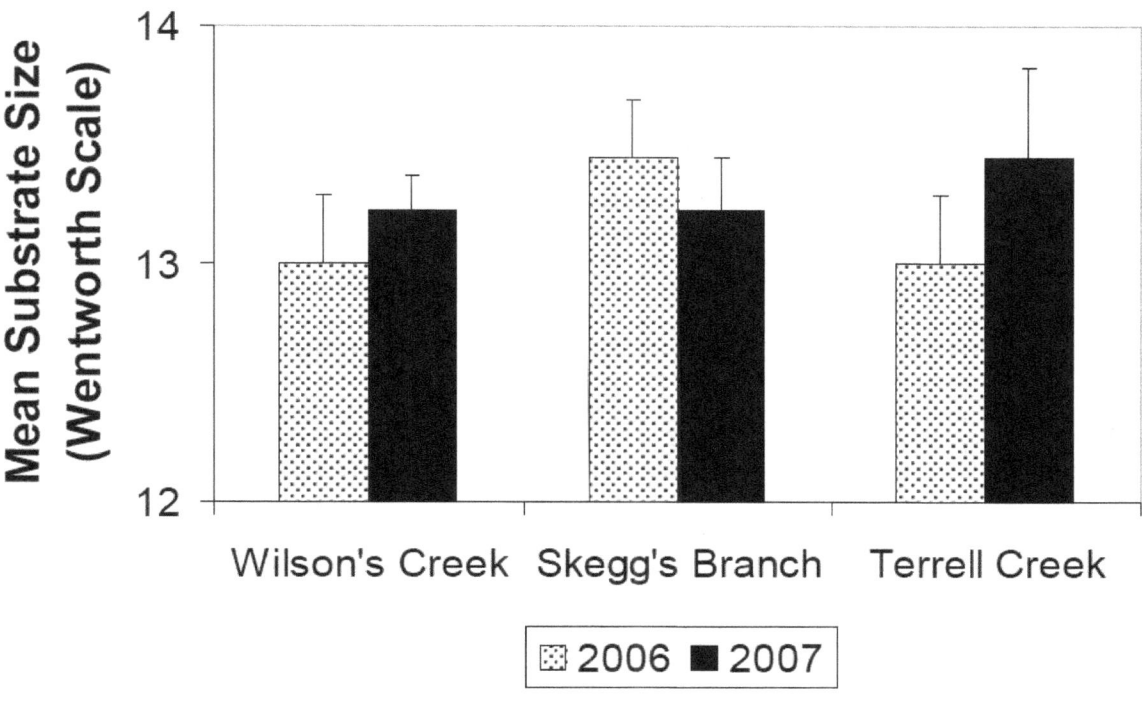

Figure 7. Mean substrate size and standard errors for stream riffles where benthic samples were collected at Wilson's Creek National Battlefield.

Table 4. Mean and standard error (in parentheses) of invertebrate metrics collected from Wilson's Creek, WICR, 1988-2007. N= number of samples collected. Hilsenhoff Biotic Index was based on family-level scores prior to 2005. Data for 2000 were collected outside the index period in the month of August.

Year	1988	1989	1990	1996	1997	1998	1999	2000	2001	2002	2003	2004	2005	2006	2007
N	10	10	10	10	10	10	10	5	10	10	10	10	10	9	9
Taxa (Genus) Richness	12 (1.4)	16.4 (0.83)	13.6 (0.2)	20.95 (1.44)	18.77 (1.79)	18.5 (1.48)	14.5 (1.12)	10.3 (0.3)	14.63 (0.61)	13.4 (0.75)	12.6 (0.78)	9.87 (1.04)	17.63 0.83)	13.56 (0.46)	14.89 (0.54)
Family Richness	10 (1)	12.5 (0.52)	9.6 (0.2)	10.8 (1.1)	12.17 (1.45)	11.8 (1)	8.93 (0.71)	5.8 (0.2)	8.57 (0.47)	8.53 (0.26)	7.73 (0.28)	7.23 (0.71)	9.97 (0.45)	9.5 (0.42)	10.78 (0.52)
EPT Richness	3.9 (0.3)	3.1 (0.68)	1.4 (0)	5.15 (0.44)	4.57 (0.84)	5.65 (0.43)	3.1 (0.71)	2.5 (0.1)	4.6 (0.2)	3.83 (0.28)	3.83 (0.51)	1.87 (0.38)	3.57 (0.22)	2.47 (0.21)	3.78 (0.52)
EPT Ratio	0.61 (0.09)	0.26 (0.03)	>0.01 (>0.01)	0.27 (0.06)	0.25 (0.08)	0.56 (0.02)	0.37 (0.1)	0.11 (0.03)	0.39 (0.02)	0.28 (0.04)	0.37 (0.13)	0.33 (0.08)	0.29 (0.04)	0.57 (0.04)	0.18 (0.03)
Shannon Index (Family)	1.47 (0.16)	1.09 (0.09)	0.72 (0.01)	1.15 (0.08)	1.23 (0.08)	1.62 (0.08)	1.27 (0.08)	0.83 (0.06)	1.45 (0.07)	1.38 (0.04)	1.35 (0.05)	1.43 (0.11)	1.42 (0.04)	n/a	n/a
Shannon Index (Genus)	1.12 (0.07)	0.22 (0.04)	1.14 (0.11)	0.90 (0.08)	1.76 (0.06)	1.09 (0.11)	1.64 (0.11)	1.44 (0.24)	1.45 (0.06)	1.35 (0.06)	1.88 (0.19)	1.49 (0.09)	1.94 (0.09)	2.03 (0.06)	1.93 (0.14)
Shannon Evenness Index	0.49 (0.03)	0.12 (0.02)	0.57 (0.08)	0.46 (0.03)	0.69 (0.03)	0.56 (0.03)	0.70 (0.07)	0.66 (0.04)	0.67 (0.03)	0.63 (0.04)	0.76 (0.09)	0.62 (0.05)	0.71 (0.05)	0.77 (0.01)	0.72 (0.05)
Hilsenhoff Biotic Index	5.33 (0.13)	5.61 (0.09)	6.61 (0.11)	5.85 (0.18)	5.94 (0.19)	5.5 (0.05)	6.17 (0.31)	6.61 (0.08)	5.77 (0.11)	5.87 (0.18)	5.83 (0.35)	5.24 (0.25)	5.98 (0.10)	5.37 (0.15)	6.72 (0.69)
Missouri Stream Condition Index	10	8	8	10	10	10	10	8	10	10	10	10	10	10	10

Table 5. Mean and standard error (in parentheses) of invertebrate metrics collected from Skegg's Branch, Wilson's Creek National Battlefield, 1988-2007. N= number of samples collected. Hilsenhoff Biotic Index was based on family-level scores prior to 2005.

Year	1988	1989	1990	1997	1999	2001	2002	2003	2004	2005	2006	2007
N	5	10	5	10	10	10	10	5	10	5	9	9
Family Richness	12	17.3	17	17.3	12.5	10.87	8	8.2	8.68	9.78	11	11.89
	n/a	(0.3)	n/a	(1.1)	(0.7)	(0.74)	(0.2)	n/a	(1)	(0.74)	(0.85)	(0.59)
Taxa (Genus) Richness	14	23.5	23.8	25.8	20	18.73	15.7	14	11.88	18.56	20	21.67
	n/a	(0.5)	n/a	(0.6)	(1.8)	(0.53)	(1.3)	n/a	(2.08)	(1.56)	(1.5)	(1.42)
EPT Richness	3.8	6.2	5.6	5.1	2.8	4.87	2.8	4.4	2.45	3	3.89	3.78
	n/a	(0.4)	n/a	(0.5)	(0.4)	(0.18)	(0.2)	n/a	(0.9)	0.37	(0.48)	(0.52)
EPT Ratio	0.72	0.55	0.58	0.27	0.29	0.45	0.33	0.45	0.44	0.36	0.28	0.18
	n/a	(0.16)	n/a	(0.03)	(0.09)	(0.02)	(0.05)	n/a	(0.1)	(0.06)	(0.04)	(0.03)
Shannon Index (Family)	1.92	1.92	1.86	1.96	1.7	1.76	1.35	1.24	1.7	0.72	n/a	n/a
	n/a	(0.02)	n/a	(0.02)	(0.09)	(0.12)	(0.07)	n/a	(0.12)	(0.04)		
Shannon Index (Genus)	n/a	1.90	1.73	1.86	1.6285	1.73	1.33	1.27	1.95	1.59	2.34	2.0
		(0.08)	(0.04)	(0.08)	(0.06)	(0.17)	(0.16)	(0.29)	(0.08)	(0.14)	(0.10)	(0.12)
Shannon Evenness Index	n/a	0.67	0.63	0.65	0.74	0.72	0.67	0.66	0.80	0.69	0.77	0.66
		(0.03)	(0.01)	(0.03)	(0.07)	(0.07)	(0.08)	(0.14)	(0.03)	(0.08)	(0.02)	(0.03)
Hilsenhoff Biotic Index	5.81	5.69	5.70	6.12	5.5	5.21	5.41	6.24	4.95	4.39	5.49	5.72
	n/a	(0.11)	n/a	(0.19)	(0.12)	(0.09)	(0.09)	n/a	(0.07)	(0.29)	(0.10)	(0.22)
Missouri Stream Condition Index	10	14	14	14	10	12	10	10	12	12	10	12

15

Table 6. Mean and standard error (in parentheses) of invertebrate metrics collected from Terrell Creek, Wilson's Creek National Battlefield, 2006-2007. N= number of samples collected.

Terrell Creek		
Year	**2006**	**2007**
N	9	9
Family Richness	15.89 (1.12)	14.78 (0.94)
Taxa (Genus) Richness	25.44 (1.99)	22.44 (1.33)
EPT Richness	7.78 (0.68)	4.56 (0.58)
EPT Ratio	0.43 (0.04)	0.15 (0.04)
Shannon Index (Genus)	2.69 (0.10)	2.19 (0.10)
Shannon Evenness Index	0.83 (0.02)	0.71 (0.03)
Hilsenhoff Biotic Index	5.00 (0.18)	5.30 (0.20)
Missouri Stream Condition Index	18	14

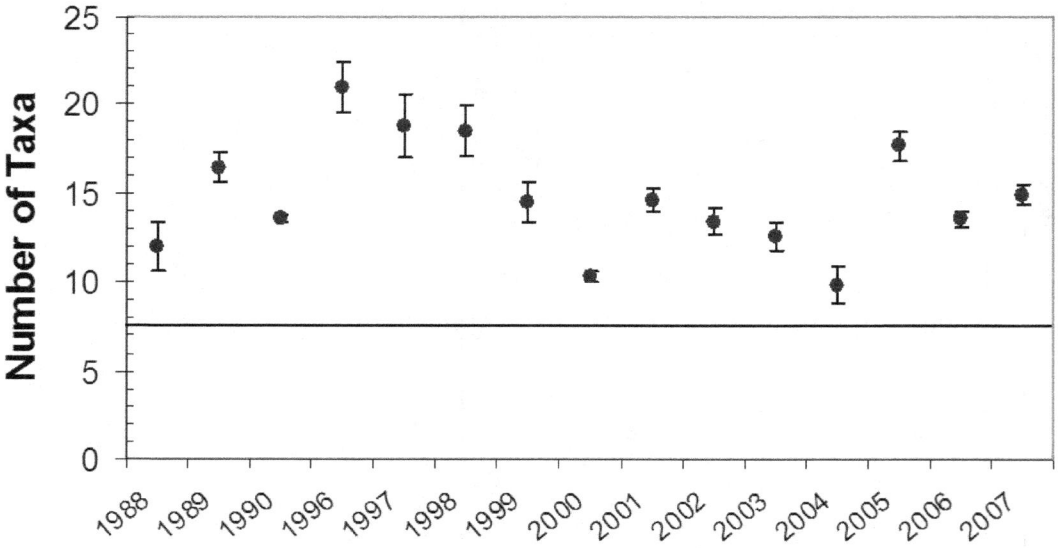

Figure 8. Control chart for taxa richness at Wilson's Creek, Wilson's Creek National Battlefield, 1988-2007. Points are means for a given sampling date, and the vertical bars are standard errors. The horizontal line represents the control limit corresponding to a 0.05 Type I error rate.

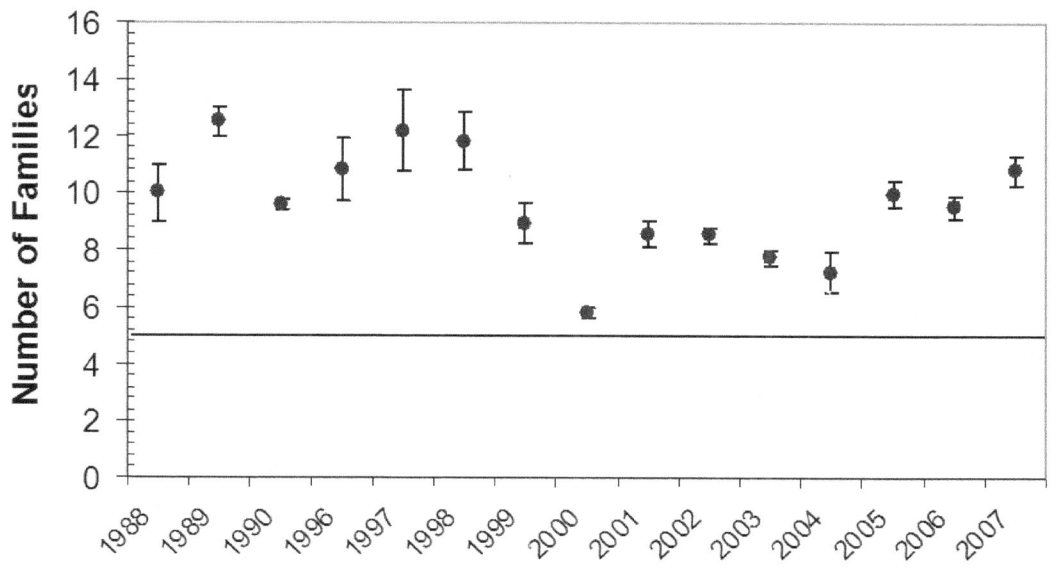

Figure 9. Control chart for family richness at Wilson's Creek, Wilson's Creek National Battlefield, 1988-2007. Points are means for a given sampling date, and the vertical bars are standard errors. The horizontal line represents the control limit corresponding to a 0.05 Type I error rate.

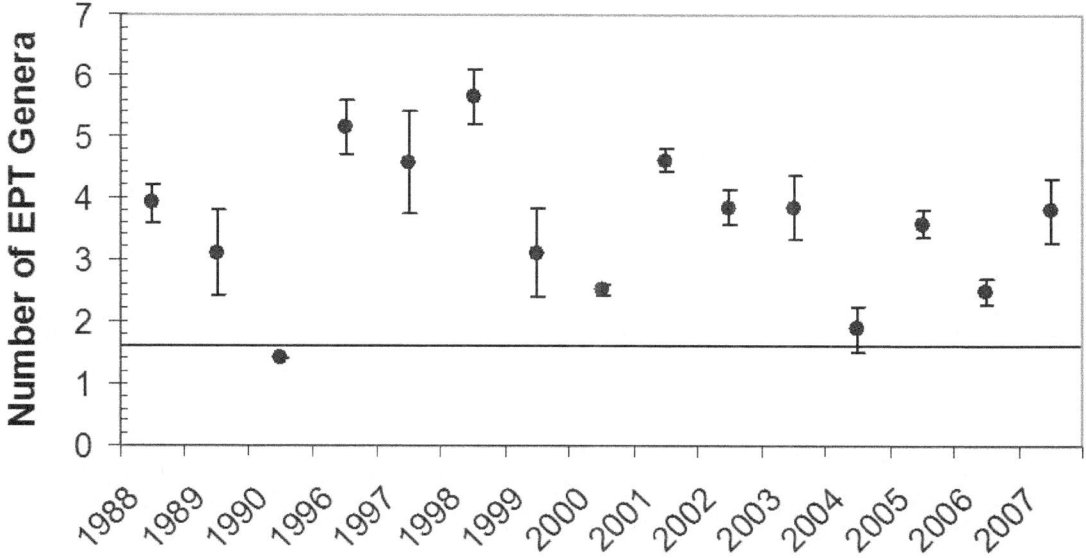

Figure 10. Control chart for Ephemeroptera, Plecoptera, and Trichoptera (EPT) at Wilson's Creek, Wilson's Creek National Battlefield, 1988-2007. Points are means for a given sampling date, and the vertical bars are standard errors. The horizontal line represents the control limit corresponding to a 0.05 Type I error rate.

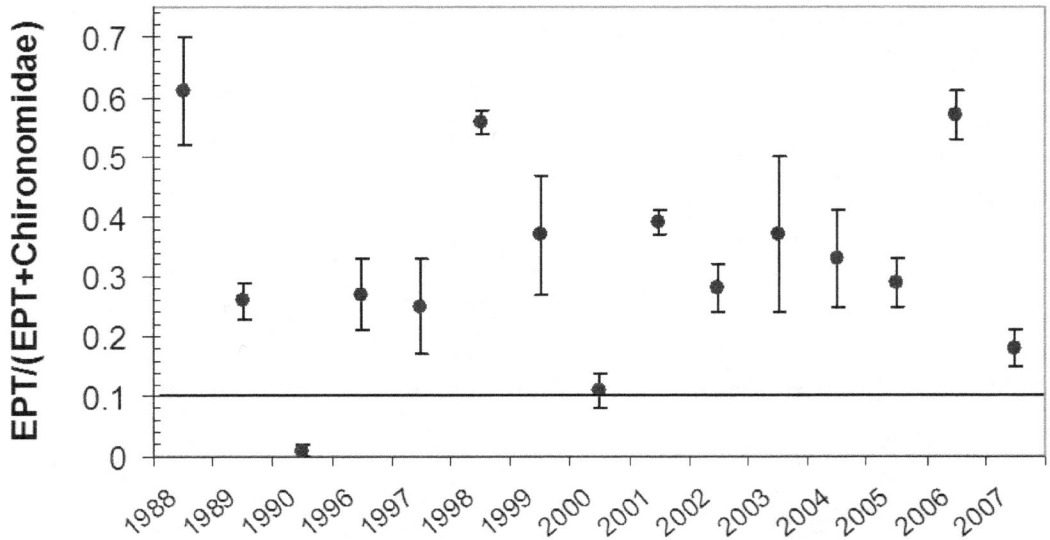

Figure 11. Control chart for EPT ratio at Wilson's Creek, Wilson's Creek National Battlefield, 1988-2007. Points are means for a given sampling date, and the vertical bars are standard errors. The horizontal line represents the control limit corresponding to a 0.05 Type I error rate.

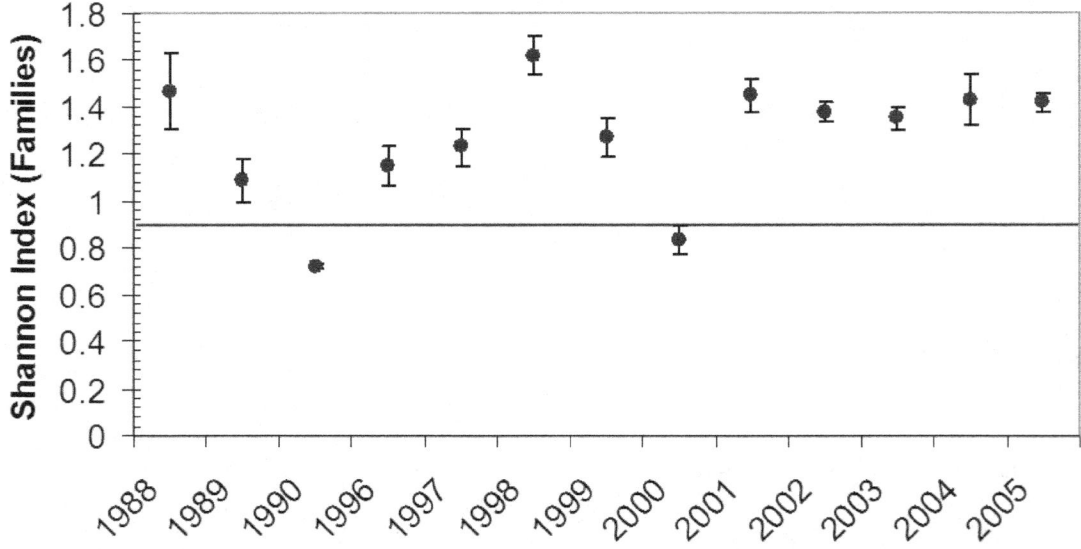

Figure 12. Control chart for Shannon Index for families at Wilson's Creek, Wilson's Creek National Battlefield, 1988-2007. Points are means for a given sampling date, and the vertical bars are standard errors. The horizontal line represents the control limit corresponding to a 0.05 Type I error rate.

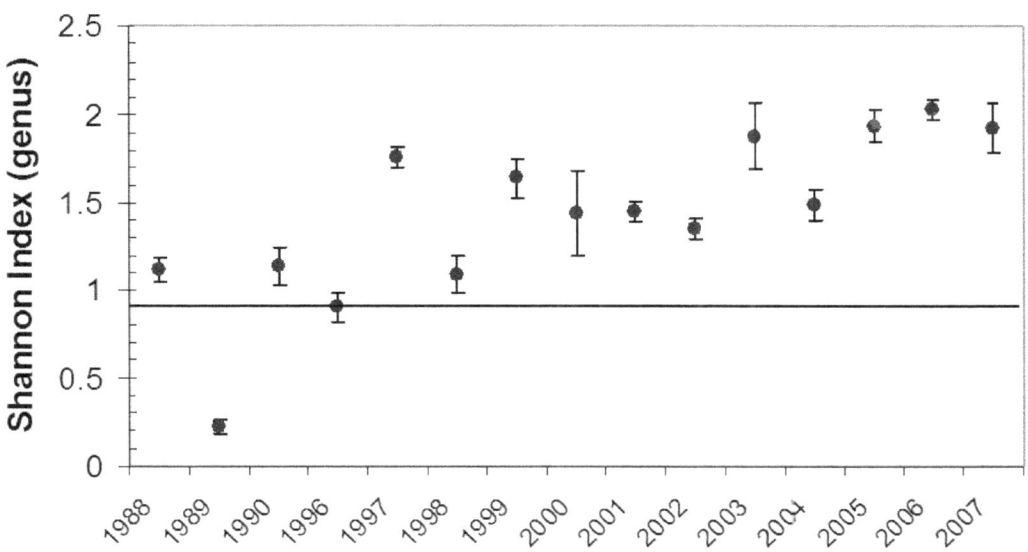

Figure 13. Control chart for Shannon Index for genera at Wilson's Creek, Wilson's Creek National Battlefield, 1988-2007. Points are means for a given sampling date, and the vertical bars are standard errors. The horizontal line represents the control limit corresponding to a 0.05 Type I error rate.

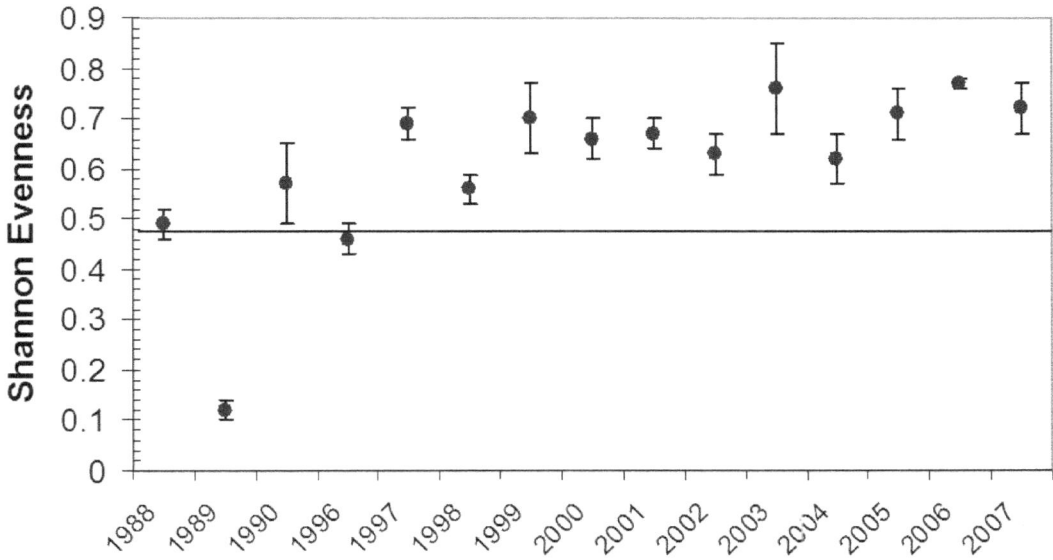

Figure 14. Control chart for Shannon Evenness Index at Wilson's Creek, Wilson's Creek National Battlefield, Missouri, 1988-2007. Points are means for a given sampling date, and the vertical bars are standard errors. The horizontal line represents the control limit corresponding to a 0.05 Type I error rate.

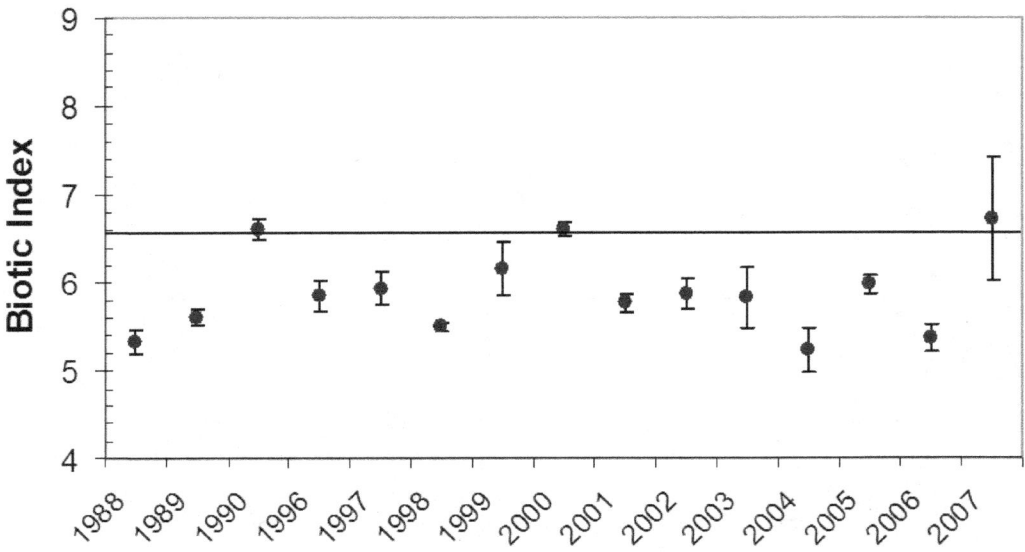

Figure 15. Control chart for Hilsenhoff Biotic Index at Wilson's Creek, Wilson's Creek National Battlefield, 1988-2007. Points are means for a given sampling date, and the vertical bars are standard errors. The horizontal line represents the control limit corresponding to a 0.05 Type I error rate. Hilsenhoff Biotic Index was based on family-level scores prior to 2005.

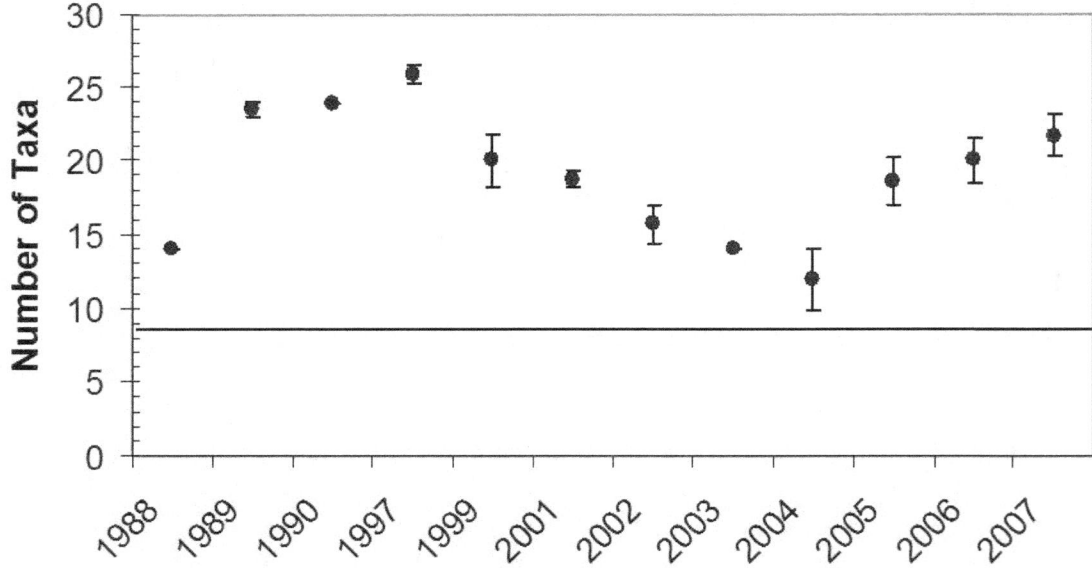

Figure 16. Control chart for taxa richness at Skegg's Branch, Wilson's Creek National Battlefield, 1988-2007. Points are means for a given sampling date, and the vertical bars are standard errors. The horizontal line represents the control limit corresponding to a 0.05 Type I error rate.

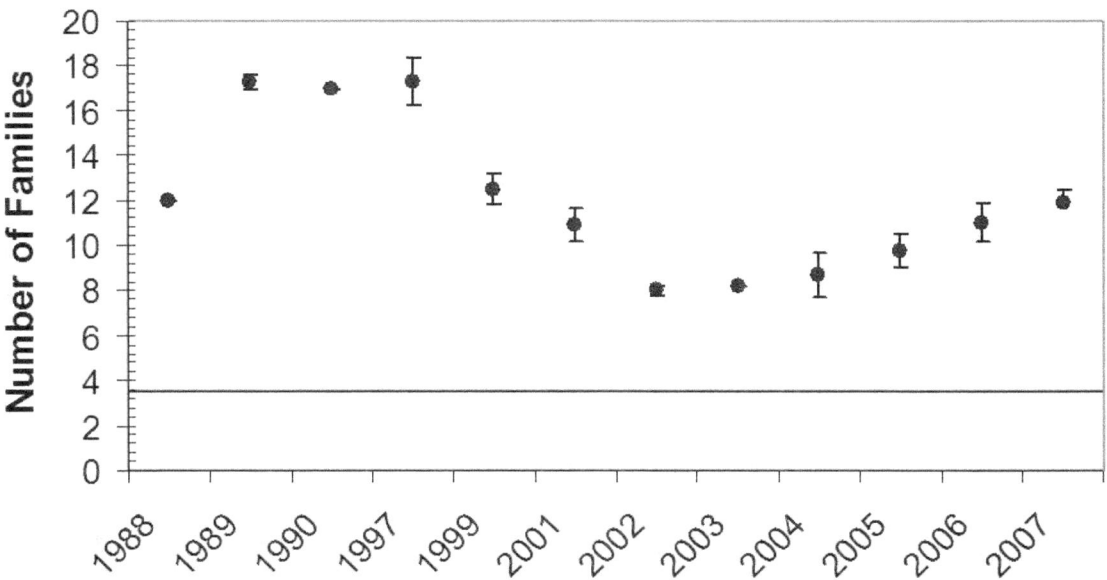

Figure 17. Control chart for family richness at Skegg's Branch, Wilson's Creek National Battlefield, 1988-2007. Points are means for a given sampling date, and the vertical bars are standard errors. The horizontal line represents the control limit corresponding to a 0.05 Type I error rate.

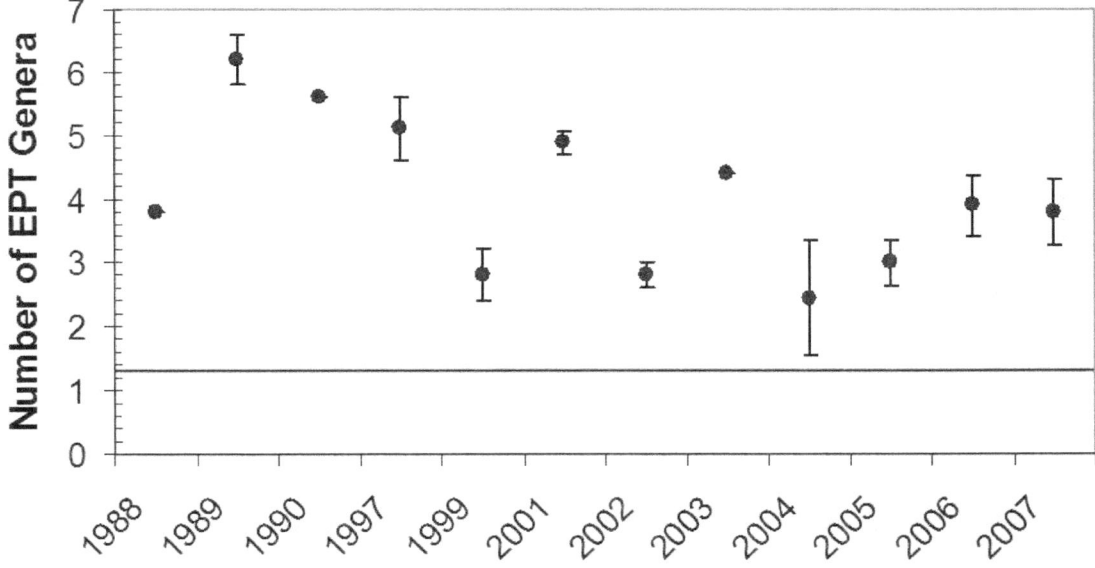

Figure 18. Control chart for Ephemeroptera, Plecoptera and Trichoptera (EPT) richness at Skegg's Branch, Wilson's Creek National Battlefield, 1988-2007. Points are means for a given sampling date, and the vertical bars are standard errors. The horizontal line represents the control limit corresponding to a 0.05 Type I error rate.

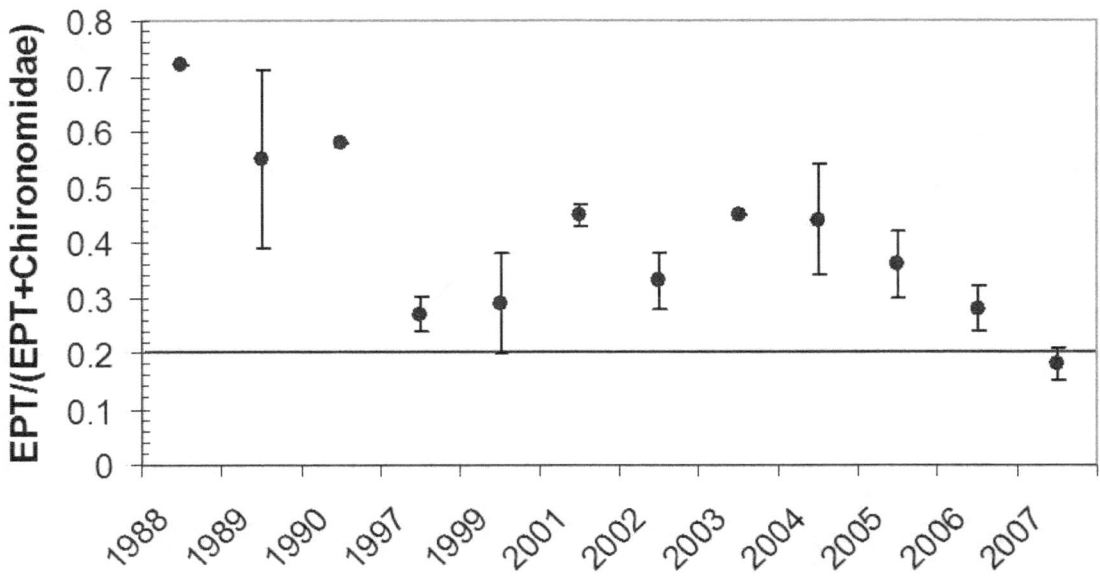

Figure 19. Control chart for EPT ratio at Skegg's Branch, Wilson's Creek National Battlefield, 1988-2007. Points are means for a given sampling date, and the vertical bars are standard errors. The horizontal line represents the control limit corresponding to a 0.05 Type I error rate.

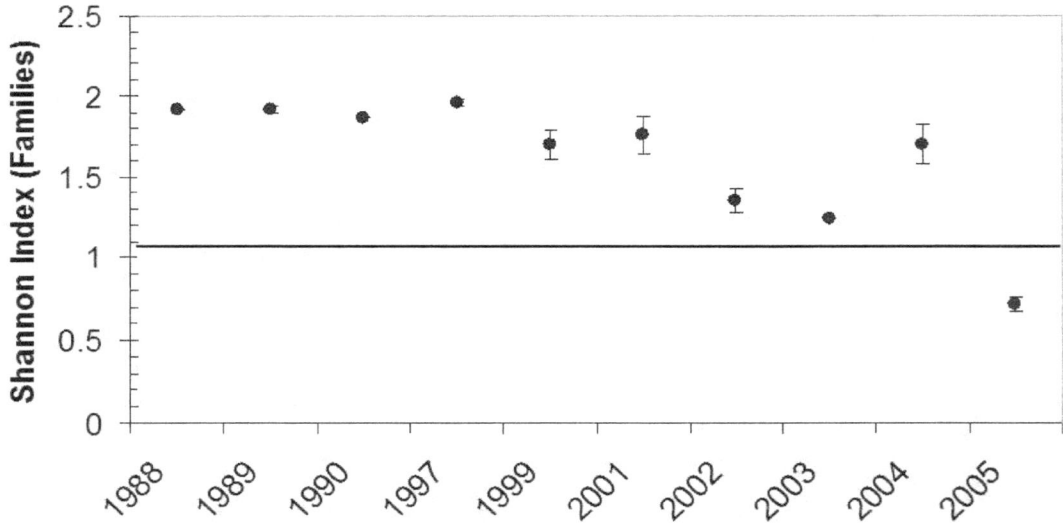

Figure 20. Control chart for Shannon Index (families) at Skegg's Branch, Wilson's Creek National Battlefield, 1988-2007. Points are means for a given sampling date, and the vertical bars are standard errors. The horizontal line represents the control limit corresponding to a 0.05 Type I error rate.

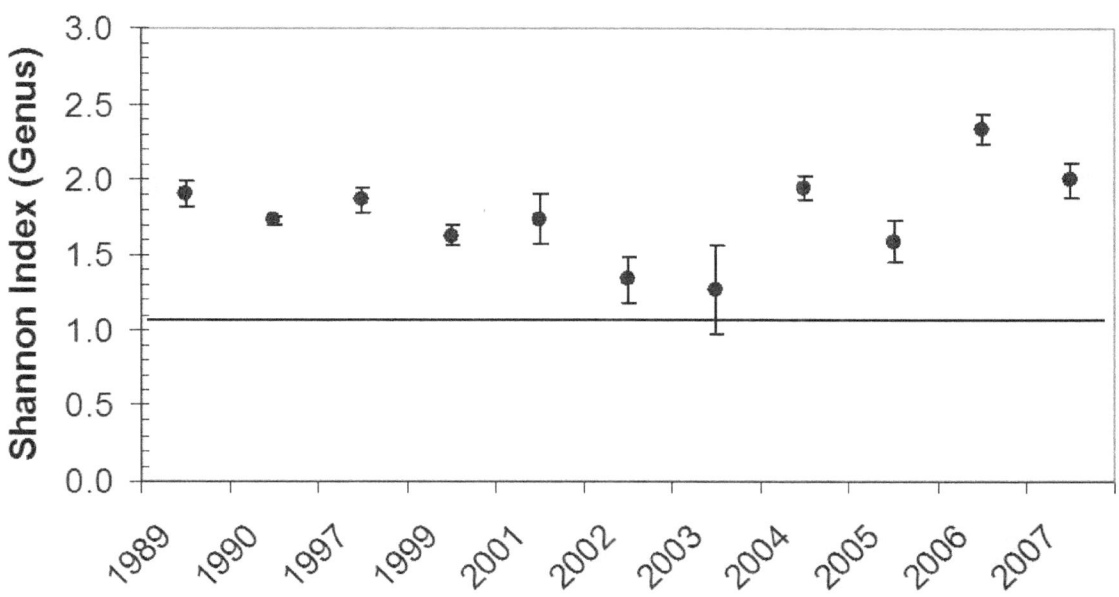

Figure 21. Control chart for Shannon Index (genera) at Skegg's Branch, Wilson's Creek National Battlefield, 1988-2007. Points are means for a given sampling date, and the vertical bars are standard errors. The horizontal line represents the control limit corresponding to a 0.05 Type I error rate.

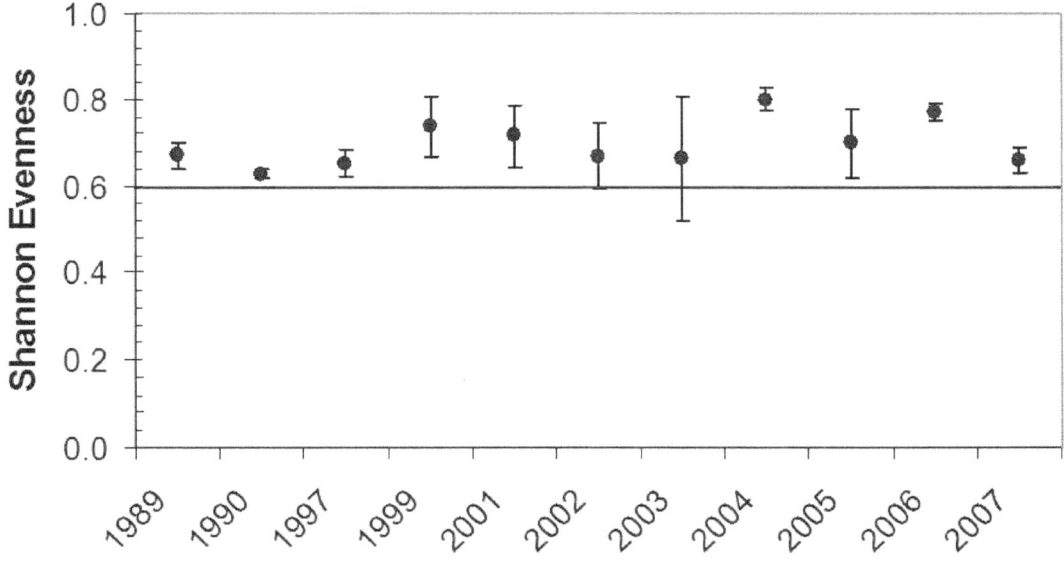

Figure 22. Control chart for Shannon Evenness Index at Skegg's Branch, Wilson's Creek National Battlefield, Missouri, 1988-2007. Points are means for a given sampling date, and the vertical bars are standard errors. The horizontal line represents the control limit corresponding to a 0.05 Type I error rate.

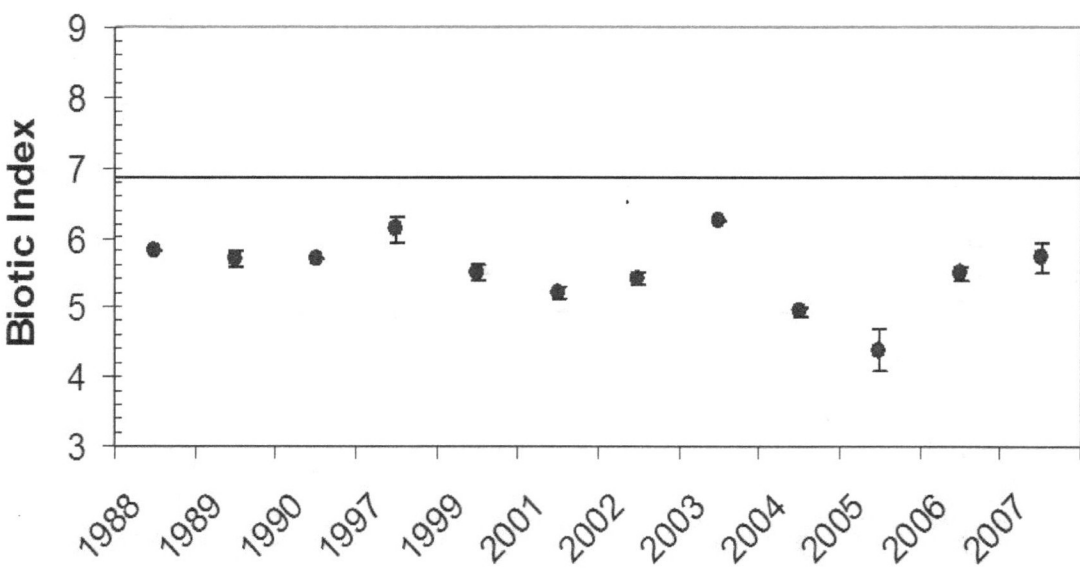

Figure 23. Control chart for Hilsenhoff's Biotic Index at Skegg's Branch, Wilson's Creek National Battlefield, Missouri, 1988-2007. Points are means for a given sampling date, and the vertical bars are standard errors. The horizontal line represents the control limit corresponding to a 0.05 Type I error rate. Hilsenhoff Biotic Index was based on family-level scores prior to 2005

Discussion

The invertebrate metrics and SCI scores presented in this report are generally comparable to those observed for other regional streams (Jones et. al. 1981, MacFarlane 1983, Harris et al. 1991, 1999, Whiles et al. 2000, Hall et al. 2003, Sarver et al. 2002, Zelt and Frankforter 2003, Kosnicki and Sites 2007, Poulton et al. 2007, Hutchens et al. 2009). Benthic samples generally contained a diverse assemblage of invertebrates commonly associated with stream communities, including mayflies (Ephemeroptera), caddisflies (Trichoptera), dragonflies and damselflies (Odonata), midges (Chironomidae), riffle beetles (Elmidae), crayfish (Decapoda), and snails (Gastropoda). Stream invertebrate communities are notoriously variable temporally and spatially so the observed variation does not necessarily reflect impairment. Annual variation in benthic communities can be influenced by a number of factors, including water chemistry, precipitation events, and changes in physical habitat. The range of variation in benthic metrics reported here is well within the expected natural range of variation (Jones et al. 1981, Kosnicki and Sites 2007, Poulton et al. 2007). However, EPT richness and the Hilsenhoff Biotic Index (HBI) tended to range lower and higher, respectively, than expected for regional streams. EPT richness and HBI represent half of the metrics used to calculate the Missouri Stream Condition Index (SCI), and this resulted in consistently low SCI scores for Wilson's Creek and Skegg's Branch. Additionally, other factors such as using a summer index period rather than a winter or spring index period may have contributed to the low SCI scores. Invertebrate communities inhabiting regional streams are dominated by more tolerant taxa during the summer due to the stressful conditions that occur during this season (i.e., higher water temperature, lower dissolved oxygen concentration, increased nutrient and sediment loads). Life history constraints also influence which taxa are more dominant. For example, sensitive EPT generally are more diverse in winter and spring due in large part to life cycle requirements (Poulton and Stewart 1991). However, such evolutionary adaptations do not necessarily reflect anthropogenic impairment.

In contrast to the SCI scores, control charts showed that invertebrate metrics for 2005-2007 generally did not exceed their respective control limits indicating the data are within the expected range of variation. EPT ratios in Skegg's Branch have decreased during the past few years and this metric exceeded the control limit in 2007. Decreasing EPT ratios indicate that pollution tolerant Chironomidae are comprising an increasingly larger portion of the benthic community in Skegg's Branch. Increases in sediments and contaminants in runoff into Skegg's Branch associated with recent development in Republic, Missouri may be starting to depress the aquatic invertebrate fauna of this stream. Housing developments in the city of Republic are located within the drainage basin of Skegg's Branch and contribute to point source and non point source pollution. Increasing impervious surfaces in and around housing developments increases contaminated runoff and alters the flow dynamics of Skegg's Branch. In general, the extant condition of the respective invertebrate communities of Skegg's Branch and Terrell Creek do not appear to be overtly degraded. In comparison to both Wilson's Creek and Skegg's Branch, Terrell Creek had higher taxa richness, EPT richness and diversity. Some variation was observed between the two sampling years at Terrell Creek, but differences in metric values among years does not necessarily reflect biological differences in benthic community structure. The higher richness and diversity values observed for Terrell Creek may be due to this stream receiving a substantial portion of its base flow from springs compared to the other streams.

Although SCI scores for Wilson's Creek show it is clearly impaired, the evidence of impairment for Skegg's Branch is less conclusive and appears to be mild. However, the data for Skegg's Branch suggests the quality of this stream is beginning decline due to development in the watershed. The quality of Terrell Creek appears to be good. Poor water quality conditions and habitat degradation in Wilson's Creek are well documented (Black 1997 Richards and Johnson 2002). The State of Missouri presently lists 29 km of Wilson's Creek as water-quality impaired under the U.S. Clean Water Act section 303(d) (Missouri Department of Natural Resources 2009; http://www.dnr.mo.gov/ENV/wpp/waterquality/303d/2009) and this impairment has contributed to the biological impoverishment of this system (Missouri Department of Natural Resources 2007, 2009. The state attributes this toxicity to non-point source pollution from urban areas and considers Wilson's Creek a high priority for development of a Total Maximum Daily Load (TDML), as required by the Clean Water Act. Additionally, the Southwest Wastewater Treatment Plant (City of Springfield, Missouri) provides most of the baseflow for Wilson's Creek. Although upgrades and improvements to the wastewater treatment plant have improved the water quality of Wilson's Creek, those improvements are insufficient to counter the prevailing urbanized conditions in the watershed. Although Wilson's Creek is impaired, the invertebrate data collected from 2005-2007 generally indicate that stream integrity has not diminished beyond that reported in earlier studies (Harris et al. 1999, Peitz and Cribbs 2005).

There are few available options to park management for mitigating water quality impairment of streams flowing through WICR largely because impacts to water quality and associated effects on the invertebrate communities originate upstream of the park boundaries. Indeed the impacts of urbanization often are so pervasive that mitigation strategies are rarely effective (Booth 2005, Bernhardt et al. 2005, Paul et al. 2009). However, maintaining and widening of riparian buffer zones along these streams in the park will aid in protecting aquatic life as well as in-stream habitat from local chemical runoff and sedimentation. Riparian buffers can be improved by restoring native grasses to areas where they occurred historically, and maintaining native trees and shrubs on stream banks. Improved buffer zones will reduce bank erosion within WICR by reducing stream velocity and the amount of water entering the streams. A reduction in impervious surfaces (sidewalks, trails and parking lot) within the park and mowing in the riparian buffers would also help to stabilize the riparian zone and in-stream habitat. The long history and continuing efforts of aquatic invertebrate monitoring at WICR provides a sound tool to recognize both deterioration and chronic decline of water quality.

Literature Cited

Berkas, W. R. 1980. Effects of urban runoff and wastewater effluent on Wilson's Creek and James River near Springfield, Missouri: U.S. Geological Survey Water-Resources Investigations Report 80–27. 31 p.

Berkas, W. R. 1982. Streamflow and water-quality conditions, Wilson's Creek and James River, Springfield area, Missouri: U.S. Geological Survey Water-Resources Investigations Report 82–26. 38 p.

Bernhardt, E.S., M. A. Palmer, J. D. Allan, G. Alexander, K. Barnas, S. Brooks, J. Carr, S. Clayton, C. Dahm, J. Follstad-Shah, D. Galat, S. Gloss, P. Goodwin, D. Hart, B. Hassett, R. Jenkinson, S. Katz, G. M. Kondolf, P. S. Lake, R. Lave, J. L. Meyer, and T. K. O'Don. 2005. Synthesizing U.S. River Restoration Efforts. Science **308**:636-637.

Black, A. A. 1997. Wilson's Creek, Greene and Christian Counties, Missouri: water quality, macroinvertebrate indices, and planning implications using GIS, based on watershed landuse and water contamination hazards. M.S. Thesis, Southwest Missouri State University, Springfield. 257 p.

Booth, D. B. 2005. Challenges and prospects for restoring urban streams: a perspective from the Pacific Northwest of North America. Journal of the North American Benthological Society **24**:724-737.

Brown, D., and J. Czarnezki. Undated. Missouri streams fact sheet—chemical monitoring. Missouri Department of Conservation. Jefferson City, Missouri. 4 p.

Bowles, D. E., M. H. Williams, H. R. Dodd, L. W. Morrison, J. A. Hinsey, C. E. Ciak, G. A. Rowell, M. D. DeBacker, and J. L. Haack. 2008. Monitoring Protocol for Aquatic Invertebrates of Small Streams in the Heartland Inventory & Monitoring Network. Natural Resource Report NPS/HTLN/NRR—2008/042. National Park Service, Fort Collins, Colorado. 147 p.

DeBacker, M. D., C. C. Young (editor), P. Adams., L. Morrison, D. Peitz, G. A. Rowell, M. Williams, and D. Bowles. 2005. Heartland Inventory and Monitoring and Prairie Cluster Prototype Monitoring Program vital signs monitoring plan. U.S. National Park Service, Heartland I&M Network and Prairie Cluster Prototype Monitoring Program, Wilson's Creek National Battlefield, Republic, Missouri. 104 p.

Emmett, L. F., J. Skelton, R. R. Luckey, D. E. Miller, T. L. Thompson. and J. W. Whitfield. 1978. Water resources and geology of the Springfield area, Missouri: Rolla, Missouri Department of Natural Resources, Division of Geology and Land Survey, Water Resources Report 34. 160 p.

Hall, D. L., B. S. Bergthold, and R. W. Sites. 2003. The influence of adjacent land use on macroinvertebrate communities of prairie streams in Missouri. Journal of Freshwater Ecology **18**:55-68.

Harris, M. A., B. C. Kondratieff, and T. P. Boyle. 1991. Invertebrate assemblages and water quality in six National Park units in the Great Plains. National Park Service, Water Resources Division, Fort Collins, Colorado.

Harris, M. A., B. C. Kondratieff, and T. P. Boyle. 1999. Macroinvertebrate community structure of three prairie streams. Journal of the Kansas Entomological Society **72**:402-425.

Hutchens, J. J., Jr., J. A. Schuldt, C. Richards, L. B. Johnson, G. E. Host, and D. H. Breneman. 2009. Multi-scale mechanistic indicators of Midwestern USA stream macroinvertebrates. Ecological Indicators **9**:1138–1150.

Jones, J. R., B. H. Tracy, J. L. Sebaugh, D. H. Hazelwood, and M. M. Smart. 1981. Biotic index for ability to assess water quality of Missouri Ozark streams. Transactions of the American Fisheries Society **110**:627-637.

Kosnicki, E., and R. W. Sites. 2007. Least-desired index for assessing the effectiveness of grass riparian filter strips in improving water quality in an agricultural region. Environmental Entomology **36**:713-724.

MacFarlane, M. B. 1983. Structure of benthic macroinvertebrate communities in a Midwestern plains stream. Freshwater Invertebrate Biology **2**:147-153.

Missouri Department of Natural Resources. 2009. Missouri 303(d) Listed Waters Available at: http://www.dnr.mo.gov/ENV/wpp/waterquality/303d/2009

Missouri Department of Natural Resources. 2007. Springfield urban streams, Clear Creek, Jordan Creek, Wilson Creek, and Galloway Creek, Greene County. Bioassessment Report. Missouri Department of Natural Resources, Jefferson City, Missouri. 32 p.

Morrison, L. W. 2007. Assessing the reliability of ecological monitoring data: Power analysis and alternative approaches. Natural Areas Journal **27**:83–91.

Morrison, L. W. 2008. The use of control charts to interpret environmental monitoring data. Natural Areas Journal **28**:66–73.

Mueller, D. K., and D. R. Helsel. 1996, Nutrients in the Nation's waters—too much of a good thing? U.S. Geological Survey Circular 1136. 24 p.

Paul,M. J., D. W. Bressler, A. H. Purcell, M. T. Barbour, E. T. Rankin, and V. H. Resh. 2009. Assessment tools for urban catchments: defining observable biological potential. Journal of the American Water Resources Association **45**:320-330.

Peitz, D. G., and J. T. Cribbs. 2005. Bio-monitoring of water quality using aquatic invertebrates and in-stream habitat and riparian condition assessments: status report for Wilson's Creek and Skegg's Branch, Wilson's Creek National Battlefield, Missouri 1988-2004. U.S. National Park Service, Heartland I&M Network and Prairie Cluster Prototype Monitoring Program, Wilson's Creek National Battlefield, Republic, Missouri. 17 p.

Peterson, J. T. 1996. Suggested Biomonitoring protocol and status of stream quality at six Great Plains National Parks. University of Missouri, Columbia. 70 p.

Peterson, J. T., W. M. Rizzo, E. D. Schneider, and G. D. Willson. 1999. Macroinvertebrate biomonitoring protocol for four prairie streams. U.S. Geological Survey, Biological Resources Division, Northern Prairie Wildlife Research Center, Missouri Field Station, University of Missouri-Columbia. 45 p.

Poulton, B. C., T. J. Rasmussen, and C. J. Lee. 2007. Assessment of biological conditions at selected stream sites in Johnson County, and Cass County and Jackson counties, Missouri, 2003 and 2004. U.S. Geological Survey Special Investigations Report 2007-5108. 78 p.

Poulton, B. C., and K. W. Stewart. 2001. The stoneflies of the Ozark and Ouachita mountains (Plecoptera). Memoirs of the American Entomological Society 38: 1-116.

Richards, J. M., and B. T. Johnson. 2002. Water Quality, Selected Chemical Characteristics, and Toxicity of Base Flow and Urban Stormwater in the Pearson Creek and Wilson's Creek Basins, Greene County, Missouri, August 1999 to August 2000. USGS Water Resources Investigations Report 02-4124. 60 p.

Sarver, R., S. Harlan, C. Rabeni, and S. Sowa. 2002. Biological Criteria for Wadeable/Perennial Streams of Missouri. Missouri Department of Natural Resources, Jefferson City, Missouri. 47 p.

Wentworth, C. K. 1922. A scale of grade and class terms for clastic sediments. Journal of Geology 30:377-392.

Whiles, M. R., B. L. Brock, A. C. Franzen, and S. C. Dinsmore, II. 2000. Stream Invertebrate Communities, Water Quality, and Land-Use Patterns in an Agricultural Drainage Basin of Northeastern Nebraska, USA. Environmental Management 26:563-576.

Zelt, R. B., and J. D. Frankforter. 2003. Water-quality assessment of the central Nebraska basins—entering a new decade. USGS Fact Sheet 013–03. US Geological Survey, Lincoln, Nebraska. 6 p.

The NPS has organized its parks with significant natural resources into 32 networks linked by geography and shared natural resource characteristics. HTLN is composed of 15 National Park Service (NPS) units in eight Midwestern states. These parks contain a wide variety of natural and cultural resources including sites focused on commemorating civil war battlefields, Native American heritage, westward expansion, and our U.S. Presidents. The Network is charged with creating inventories of its species and natural features as well as monitoring trends and issues in order to make sound management decisions. Critical inventories help park managers understand the natural resources in their care while monitoring programs help them understand meaningful change in natural systems and to respond accordingly. The Heartland Network helps to link natural and cultural resources by protecting the habitat of our history.

The I&M program bridges the gap between science and management with a third of its efforts aimed at making information accessible. Each network of parks, such as Heartland, has its own multi-disciplinary team of scientists, support personnel, and seasonal field technicians whose system of online databases and reports make information and research results available to all. Greater efficiency is achieved through shared staff and funding as these core groups of professionals augment work done by individual park staff. Through this type of integration and partnership, network parks are able to accomplish more than a single park could on its own.

The mission of the Heartland Network is to collaboratively develop and conduct scientifically credible inventories and long-term monitoring of park "vital signs" and to distribute this information for use by park staff, partners, and the public, thus enhancing understanding which leads to sound decision making in the preservation of natural resources and cultural history held in trust by the National Park Service.

www.nature.nps.gov/im/units/htln/

Heartland Network

Natural Resource Monitoring

The Department of the Interior protects and manages the nation's natural resources and cultural heritage; provides scientific and other information about those resources; and honors its special responsibilities to American Indians, Alaska Natives, and affiliated Island Communities.

NPS 410/101120, February 2010